FORCES

AND

MOVEMENT

Peter Riley

FRANKLIN WATTS
LONDON•SYDNEY

To my granddaughter, Tabitha Grace.

First published in 2015 by
Franklin Watts
338 Euston Road
London NW1 3BH

Franklin Watts Australia
Level 17/207 Kent Street
Sydney NSW 2000

Copyright images © Franklin Watts 2015
Copyright text © Peter Riley 2015
(Some content has previously appeared in *Straightforward Science:
Forces* (2003) but has been comprehensively reworked and redesigned,
with additional content, in line with the National Curriculum for Science.)

HB ISBN 978 1 4451 3553 3
Library ebook ISBN 978 1 4451 3554 0

Dewey classification number: 531

A CIP catalogue record for this book is available from the British Library.

Editor: Julia Bird
Designer: Mo Choy Design
Printed in China

Photo acknowledgements: AG Photos/Shutterstock: 8bl. Aspen Photo/Shutterstock: 23b. Jez Bennett/
Shutterstock: 8r. Blulz60/Shutterstock: 7t. Rich Carey/Shutterstock: 16b. Donald Davis/NASA/Ames: 12b.
Digital Media Pro/Shutterstock: 4b. Digital Storm Cinema/Dreamstime: 5t. Dorling Kindersley/UIG/SPL: 10r.
Dragon Images/Shutterstock: 27b. Dreamframer/Shutterstock: 19b. FCG/Shutterstock: 6r. Flynt/Dreamstime:
14t. Angelo Giampiccolo/Shutterstock: 17t. Gotjee/Dreamstime: 18b. Joseph Gough/Dreamstime: 25r. Chris
Hill/Shutterstock: 28l. Stefan Holm/Shutterstock: 3. IM Photo/Shutterstock: front cover, 1. Dmitry Kalinovsky/
Shutterstock: 22b. Katey 997/Dreamstime: 16t. Grzegorz Kordus/Dreamstime: 19t. Robyn Mackenzie/
Dreamstime: 27t. Mediagram/Shutterstock: 2, 9br. Monkey Business Images/Dreamstime: 21b. NASA: 9l.
Natursports/Shutterstock: 13t. Orla/Shutterstock: 29b. Luril Osadchi/Shutterstock: 12t. Photographerlondon/
Dreamstime: 6l, 31r. Pindiyath100/Dreamstime: 5b. PRILL/Shutterstock: 4t. Rivtal 2012/Dreamstime: 24t.
Fouad A.Saad/Shutterstock: 10l. Sedlacek/Shutterstock: 11r. Shargaljit/Dreamstime: 24b. steamroller blues/
Shutterstock: 23t. Stocksnapper/Shutterstock: 15. Tache Photo/Shutterstock: 20t. Udeyismail/Shutterstock:
13b. Becky Wass/Shutterstock: 7b. World History Archive/Alamy: 29tr.

Every attempt has been made to clear copyright. Should there be any inadvertent omission,
please apply to the Publishers for rectification.

Franklin Watts is a division of Hachette Children's Books, an Hachette UK company.
www.hachette.co.uk

FSC
www.fsc.org
MIX
Paper from
responsible sources
FSC® C104740

Contents

Pushing and pulling

A force is a push or a pull. You cannot see a force, but you can see and feel its effects. You see the effect of the wind's force as leaves move on a tree for example, or feel its effect as the air pushes against your skin.

EXERTING FORCES

The word exerted is used to describe how a force is made. We say that wind exerts a force when it blows the leaves. You exert a force on this page when you turn it.

❚ You can see the force of the wind blowing these dandelion seeds away from the flower.

❚ This boy is using his muscles to exert a force to kick this football.

FORCES IN ACTION

Pushes and pulls move things. Once something is moving, a pull or a push may be exerted to change its direction and speed – or to stop it altogether. For example, you may use a bat to change the direction of a ball.

ENERGY

The power to exert forces comes from energy. Your muscles get their energy from the food that you eat. Engines get their energy from fuels such as petrol or diesel.

MOVEMENT

Without forces, there would be no movement. When muscles work, they exert forces that pull on your bones and move your limbs, letting you run, walk and swim. Engines exert forces to move cars, trucks, ships, submarines and spacecraft.

▌ The engine is pushing this race car along at great speed.

▌ The people on this fairground ride are feeling the effect of lots of pulls and pushes.

INVESTIGATE

Work out when you are pushing and pulling. Begin by closing this book and opening it again. When did you push? When did you pull? Try other activities and decide when you are pushing and when you are pulling.

Gravity

All large objects in space, such as the Earth, have gravity. This is a force which they exert and which pulls other objects towards their surface. The larger the size of the object, the stronger the force of gravity.

THE PULL OF GRAVITY

You feel the effect of gravity if you lose your balance – you fall over! If you throw a ball up into the air, the force you exert pushes the ball up. The ball continues to rise until the effect of gravity becomes stronger than the force of your throw. Gravity pulls the ball down towards the Earth.

▌ The force of gravity has pulled this bicycle and its rider to the ground.

▌ Gravity pulls the diver down below the water's surface.

I A tennis player has to hit the ball hard so that it travels over the net before falling towards the ground.

THROWING AND CATCHING

If you throw a ball horizontally, it does not move in a straight line through the air. As it travels forwards, gravity pulls on the ball and makes it fall. The ball gets lower and lower until it hits the ground.

For this reason, when you throw a ball to a friend, you usually throw the ball up in the direction of your friend. If you have thrown the ball high enough and hard enough, gravity will pull the ball down in time for your friend to catch it.

INVESTIGATE

Throw a ball to a friend. Keep moving further apart and throwing the ball to each other. See how high you have to throw the ball for each of you to catch it.

Weight

Everything around you, including your body, is made of a substance called matter. Matter may be a solid, such as rock, a liquid, such as water, or a gas, such as oxygen. The amount of matter in something is called its mass. The force of gravity pulls down on the mass of the solid, liquid or gas and gives it a force called weight. The weight presses down on the Earth.

WEIGHT AND MASS

The weight of something depends on its mass. An object with a small amount of mass has a small weight. An object with a large amount of mass has a large weight.

▌The African elephant has the greatest mass of all land animals – and the greatest weight!

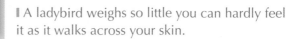

▌A ladybird weighs so little you can hardly feel it as it walks across your skin.

WEIGHT AND GRAVITY

The Moon is smaller than the Earth so it has a smaller force of gravity. When astronauts visit the Moon, they weigh six times less than they do on Earth. They still have the same mass as they had on Earth because their bodies do not change. Only the pulling force of gravity on them has changed.

❚ Gravity is much weaker on the Moon than on the Earth but it still pulls the astronaut towards its surface.

USING A BALANCE

The weight of two different things can be compared by using a balance. The two objects are placed on the trays of the balance. If the objects have the same weight, each end is pushed down with the same force and the balance stays horizontal. If one object weighs more than the other, it pushes more strongly on the balance than the other object and the balance becomes tilted.

❚ The weights on this balance weigh different amounts, so the balance is tilted.

INVESTIGATE

Hang a wire coat hanger on a bar. Now tie two empty yogurt pots of the same size to its ends. Put an object in each pot. Can you find two objects which weigh the same, so that the coat hanger stays horizontal?

Measuring force

Springs can be used to measure forces. When a force pulls on a spring, the spring stretches. If the force is made larger, the spring gets longer.

Different weights stretch springs by different amounts.

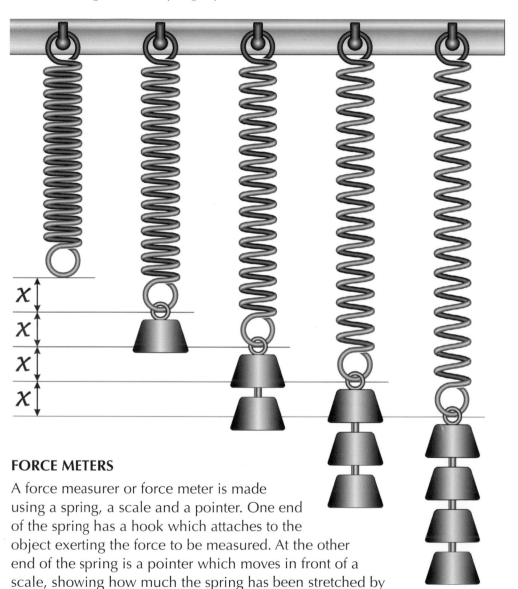

A force meter

FORCE METERS

A force measurer or force meter is made using a spring, a scale and a pointer. One end of the spring has a hook which attaches to the object exerting the force to be measured. At the other end of the spring is a pointer which moves in front of a scale, showing how much the spring has been stretched by the force.

STRETCHING

Force meters made to measure small forces use a weak spring which stretches a large amount when a small force pulls on it. A force meter which measures large forces uses a strong spring. It only stretches a tiny amount when it is pulled by a small force, but stretches greatly when pulled by a large force.

Number of marbles	Distance elastic band stretches (cm)
1 marble	
2 marbles	
3 marbles	
4 marbles	
5 marbles	

WEIGHING MACHINES

Force meters can be used to measure weight. In science the unit to measure force is called the Newton (N) after the scientist Isaac Newton (1642–1707). He is believed to have had his ideas about the force of gravity while watching an apple fall from a tree (see p.29). On the Newton scale the weight of an average apple is 1 N. Weighing machines such as bathroom and kitchen scales measure weight in kilograms or pounds. The number shown by the pointer on the weighing machine records the amount of matter in an object.

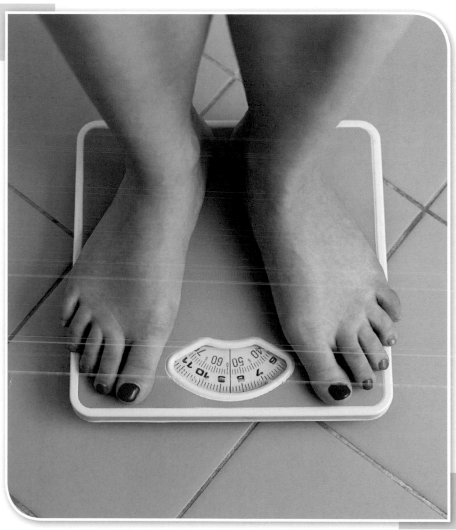

❙ Bathroom scales measure weight using a spring which is squashed by the weight placed on top of it.

11

On the move

I f an object is not moving, the forces acting on it balance. The object's weight is balanced by the upward push from the ground under it. If the object is pushed or pulled from just one end, it starts to move. This is because there is no pushing or pulling force on the other end to balance it.

MOVING IN SPACE

In space, a moving object will keep going in a straight line long after the pushing or pulling force has been removed. If the object passes close to a planet or the Sun, their force of gravity pulls on the object. The force of gravity may pull the object into an orbit.

I This bobsleigh team are pushing hard from one end before climbing in to start their run. They are providing the bobsleigh with the power to make it move.

I In 1995, the *Galileo* spacecraft went into orbit around the planet Jupiter. It was pulled into orbit by Jupiter's gravity.

SPEED AND DIRECTION

A moving object can receive extra pulls and pushes. These may make it go faster or slower, or even stop it altogether. It can also be pushed from the side to make it change direction. A stronger force has a greater effect on a moving object than a weaker force. It will make an object speed up or slow down faster – or change direction more quickly – than a weaker force.

INVESTIGATE

Kick a football and run after it. Kick it again to speed it up, then try to slow it down. What force do you use to stop it?

❙ This player has been pushed off the ball as he runs forwards.

GOING FORWARD

When you push or pull on something in one direction, a force is exerted in the opposite direction. It is equal in strength to the force you have exerted and is called a reaction force. When someone rows a boat, the oars push the water backwards. A reaction force from the water of the same size, but acting in the opposite direction, pushes the boat forwards.

❙ As the water is pushed backwards, the rowing boat is pushed forwards.

Friction

All surfaces, even smooth ones, have tiny projections which lock together when one surface is placed on another. They create a force called friction.

I The pattern of grooves on the sole of a trainer make a rough surface to increase friction and give better grip.

I When this book is pushed along a table, sliding friction develops between the two surfaces.

HOW IT WORKS

Friction develops when one surface is pushed or pulled over another one. There are two main kinds of friction – static friction and sliding friction. You can see friction in action with the following activity. Place a book on a table. When the book's surface is gently pushed over the table, the book does not move because static friction pushes back from the surface of the table with equal strength.

MOVING FRICTION

If you push the book with a greater force, it overcomes static friction, and the book starts to move over the table. The projections still exert a force on the moving surface. This is called sliding friction and it pushes in the opposite direction. If you stop pushing the book there is only sliding friction pushing on the book and this makes the book stop moving.

SKIDDING

The wheel of a car or other vehicle is moved by receiving a turning force from the engine. There is friction between the tyre and road surface. This lets the tyre grip the road and allows the turning force to push on the road. The pushing force moves the wheel and the vehicle along. A skid happens when the friction between the tyre and the road is lost and the tyre slides over the road surface. Rain and ice can cause skidding because they fill the gaps in the rough road surface and make it smoother so the force of friction is reduced.

OIL AND FRICTION

At the axle of a bicycle wheel, metal surfaces rub together. The friction between the surfaces slows down the turning wheel. Oil is used to make a layer to separate the surfaces, reducing the friction and making the wheel turn more easily.

❙ In wet weather, deep grooves, called tread, help to spray water away from a tyre's surface, helping the vehicle to grip the road.

INVESTIGATE

Find a tray and tip it to make a ramp. Slide small objects such as wooden or plastic blocks down it. Compare the amount of friction there is between them and the tray.

Water resistance

It is hard work walking through water. As you move, you push on the water but the water pushes back on you with a force called water resistance.

HIGH RESISTANCE

The size of the water resistance depends on the shape of the object moving through the water. Imagine walking in water holding a suitcase in front of you. The water piles up in front of its large, flat surface and pushes even harder. This makes the water resistance very high.

❚ You can feel water resistance on your feet and ankles when you paddle through water.

STREAMLINED FISH

Water resistance is reduced if the object moving through the water has a streamlined shape. This shape has a point at the front, with a gently curving body spreading out from the point, then tapering to a point at the other end. Most fish have streamlined bodies so their muscles can move them easily through the water.

❚ The streamlined bodies of fish means they use little effort to swim a long way.

▌This speedboat has a pointed hull with a curved, smooth surface which reduces water resistance so the speedboat can move quickly through the water.

BOATS

Water resistance acts on the surface, too. If a boat is pointed at the front, water will pass under it easily and offer little water resistance. This means the boat can travel fast over the water. Water pushes harder on a boat with a flat front and makes it move more slowly.

INVESTIGATE

You can investigate shapes and streamlining in the following way. Fill tall plastic jars with non-allergenic wallpaper paste and water to make a thick liquid. Pinch off modelling clay into lumps of about one centimetre across. Make them into different shapes, such as a ball, tear drop, pancake and square block, then time how long they take to sink in the jars. Show your results in a table. What do you conclude?

Moving through air

As we have seen, a boat moving through water has water resistance acting against it. In a similar way, an object moving through air has a force called air resistance working against it.

PUSHY AIR

Air is a mixture of gases such as oxygen, nitrogen and carbon dioxide. As you move around the mixture of gases flows over you and pushes on you. It is so weak that you do not notice it. But if you run around holding a sheet of cardboard, for example, you will notice the strength of the air resistance as the air piles up in front of the cardboard and pushes harder.

VEHICLES

The shape of a vehicle affects the amount of air resistance, or drag, on the vehicle. Curved surfaces, such as on the body of a sports car, allow the air to flow easily over an object and the air resistance is low. This means that the car can travel faster. Vans and lorries have flat, vertical surfaces. As they move along, these surfaces push on the air. The air pushes back on them before slowly moving around the sides. This makes the air resistance much higher and means that vans and lorries travel more slowly.

❚ The front of a sports car is shaped like the wedge of a knife blade to cut through the air. Its other surfaces are curved to let the air flow past smoothly and keep air resistance low.

The curved helmet and crouching position reduce air resistance so the cyclist can move quickly.

TRAVELLING AT SPEED

At low speeds, such as walking speed, the force of air resistance is weak. But as the speed of the object increases, air resistance increases too. For this reason, racing cyclists who wish to travel fast wear streamlined helmets, and runners wear skin-tight clothes.

USING AIR RESISTANCE

Air resistance can be used to our advantage. When sky divers jump, gravity pulls them down to the Earth. They open their parachutes to increase the air resistance so they can make a safe landing.

INVESTIGATE

Make two toy parachutes out of cloth, string and weights. Use a larger piece of cloth for one and compare how fast each one falls.

The air resistance on a parachute slows down the sky diver's fall.

Simple machines

When you think of a machine you probably think about something complicated like a washing machine or car engine, but some machines are very simple, such as a ramp.

MACHINES AND WORK

To understand why some machines can be simple we have to think about what a machine does. A machine is something that makes work easier to do. We all have our ideas about what the word work means, but in science it means this: work equals the force (or effort) exerted on an object multiplied by the distance the force is used.

I A go-kart engine is a complicated machine, but its wheels are an example of a simple machine.

WORK = FORCE (EFFORT) X DISTANCE FORCE IS USED

20

HARD AND EASY

Hard work is when you use a great force over a short distance. Lifting a heavy load straight up is an example of this. The work becomes easier when you push the same load up a ramp to get to the same height. This means that the ramp is a simple machine because it makes work easier.

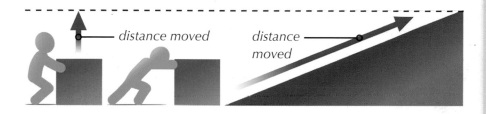

distance moved

distance moved

❚ Increasing the distance moved by using the ramp lowers the force and effort required, and makes the work easier to do.

INVESTIGATE

You can investigate the size of the force used in raising an object straight up as opposed to using a ramp in the following way. Attach a force meter to an object and raise it 10 cm. Place the object at the bottom of a ramp and pull on it with the force meter to raise it to a height of 10 cm. You should find that the force needed to pull the object up the ramp is smaller than the force needed to raise it vertically. Try this experiment with long and short ramps. How does the force change?

❚ Using a ramp makes it easier to get this wheelchair onto a bus.

Levers

A lever is another simple machine. Two forces act on it. They are called the load and the effort. There is a place on the lever where the forces cause the lever to turn. This point is called the pivot. There are three types or classes of lever.

FIRST CLASS LEVERS

In a first class lever, the load and effort are on different sides of the pivot. A crow bar is an example of a first class lever. It is used to raise large, heavy objects, such as rocks or fallen tree trunks.

❚ This crow bar is being used to lift some building slabs.

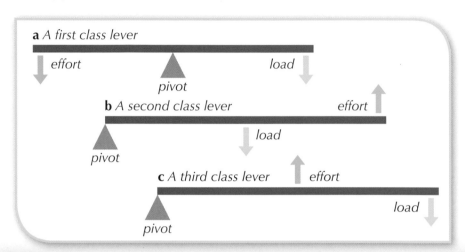

a *A first class lever*

effort   pivot   load

b *A second class lever*   effort

pivot   load

c *A third class lever*   effort

pivot   load

effort

load   pivot

SECOND CLASS LEVERS

With a second class lever, the load and effort are found on the same side of the pivot. The load is nearer the pivot than the effort. The effort moves upwards a long way to raise the load and makes the work easier to do. A wheelbarrow is an example of a second class lever.

load

effort

pivot

I Lifting the handles raises the load off the ground so it is ready to be pushed along.

THIRD CLASS LEVERS

In third class levers, the load and effort applied are on the same side of the pivot. The effort is nearer the pivot than the load. A baseball bat is an example of a third class lever. The pivot is the grip of the hands, the effort is the push of the muscles on the arm, the load is the baseball at the end of the bat being knocked away.

INVESTIGATE

Your arm is a third class lever. Measure the change in length of your arm muscle as you raise your arm, then measure the change in height of your hand to show how a little work from a muscle produces a large movement.

I The player uses the bat to hit the ball as far as he can.

pivot

load

effort

Winch, beam and pulley

The winch, beam and pulley are examples of simple machines. They are all used to make lifting loads easier. Sometimes the use of one machine leads to the development of another, for example the beam lead to the development of the more efficient pulley.

WINCHES

The pivot is at the centre of a winch. The bent handle or crank is the lever. Winches are used at wells to raise buckets of water. When the crank handle is turned, the effort force moves a long way round in a circle. This makes the centre move round with greater force and raises the bucket of water. A much smaller force is needed to raise the bucket than if it was simply pulled up on a rope. This means the winch makes work much easier.

BEAMS

You can lift a heavy object by pulling on a rope over a beam. You can use your weight as well as your strength to help you. Some of the force you exert is used to pull against the force of friction between the rope and the beam. This does not make the beam a good lifting device, but it did lead to the invention of the pulley.

❚ A winch makes lifting a heavy bucket of water at a well easier to do.

❚ Beams are made of strong materials, such as metal or wood.

PULLEYS

A pulley is a wheel used to make lifting using ropes easier. A rope moves over a wheel and turns it so that friction is reduced as a weight is raised or lowered. Pulleys can be connected together in groups to help lift very heavy objects such as car engines.

INVESTIGATE

Make this simple pulley and winch. Pulley: put a cotton reel onto a pencil and attach the pencil to two chairs with sticky tape. Winch: make a winch support from cardboard and glue. Put a cotton reel onto a bendy plastic straw, secure it with modelling clay, then place it in the holes in the support. Bend the flexible end of the plastic straw to make the handle. Attach one end of a piece of thread to the reel with sticky tape. Attach a weight made from modelling clay one centimetre across to the other end and hang it over the pulley. Raise the weight on the pulley, then put the thread over the pencil (the beam). Raise it again and compare the results.

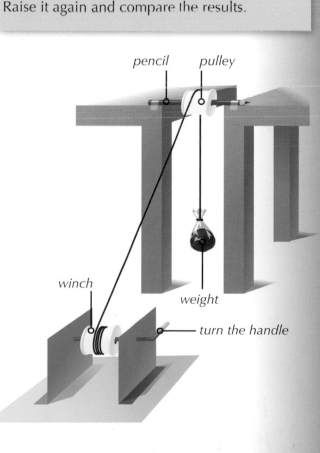

pencil   pulley

winch

weight

turn the handle

Gears

A gear is a wheel with teeth around its edge. It is sometimes called a cog wheel. Two gear wheels are needed to form a simple machine. Their teeth must interlock so that when one turns, it causes the other to turn too. Gears are found in a wide range of machines, from clocks and food mixers to cars and sewing machines.

HOW GEARS WORK

Gears are very useful in machines. Here are two gear wheels in a model. When you turn one wheel, the other wheel moves in the opposite direction. Gear wheels can be used to change the direction of a force. In some machines, such as the gear box of a car, a range of gear wheels of different sizes is used.

❙ The teeth of a gear wheel interlock to make a simple machine.

❙ When one wheel turns, the other moves in the opposite direction.

SPEED AND FORCE

Gear wheels of different sizes are used to either increase speed or increase force. In the following pictures one wheel is used to drive the other. The drive wheel may get its power from a car engine or a cyclist pushing down on the pedals.

A

❙ In picture A the blue wheel is the drive wheel. As it turns, it makes the green wheel turn around twice as fast. This gear arrangement is used to increase the speed of a moving car or bicycle. The gear which increases the speed of a moving car or bicycle is called a high gear.

B

❙ In picture B the green wheel is the drive wheel. The force applied to the blue wheel makes it turn round more slowly than the green wheel, but with much greater force. This force is used to push the wheels of a stationary car or bicycle to get it moving. The gear which increases the pushing power is called a low gear.

WHISKS

Gears can interlock in different ways, as in a hand rotary food whisk. When the handle is turned, the gears change the direction and speed of the turning movement to whisk the food.

❚ The gears interlock next to the lower handle of this whisk.

BICYCLE CHAINS

Gear wheels can be connected together by a chain, as shown in a bicycle. When this is done, the gear wheels turn in the same direction. They also have two main uses. They are used to increase the turning speed of the back wheel on a flat road and the pushing force of the back wheel when climbing a hill.

❚ The axle of this bike's back wheel has a range of different sized gears to help the cyclist move quickly and to climb hills.

INVESTIGATE
Compare how the back wheel moves when you change the gears on a bicycle.

Galileo and Newton

The force we are most aware of is the pull of gravity. If we let something go, gravity pulls it down. The study of forces really began when scientists started to measure them. The measurements provided data that allowed scientists to make calculations and predictions about how objects move when forces act upon them.

I Galileo is often described as the father of modern science.

GREEK IDEAS

The Ancient Greeks (8th century BCE – 2nd century BCE) were among the first to explore forces. The Ancient Greeks believed an object fell because it contained a substance called earth that was attracted to the earth in the ground. They thought heavier objects fell faster because they contained more earth.

GALILEO MAKES PROGRESS

Galileo Galilei (1564–1642) was an Italian scientist. A story tells of him dropping cannon balls off the leaning tower of Pisa to study falling. He really used ramps and timed how long it took for balls of different weights to roll down them. He found that all the balls took the same time to reach the bottom of the ramp so the Ancient Greeks' idea about earth was disproved. He also found that the balls went faster and faster as they rolled down the ramps. They accelerated as if there was a pulling force acting on them all the time. We now call this pulling force gravity.

INVESTIGATE

Find two balls of the same size, but different weights, and let them roll down a ramp. They should arrive at the bottom together, but repeat the experiment a few times to check.

NEWTON AND GRAVITY

Isaac Newton was an English scientist. He studied Galileo's work and wondered how gravity could be explained. It is said that he had an idea when looking at the Moon and seeing an apple fall from a tree. He knew that gravity made the apple fall, but also believed it made the Moon fall around the Earth. He made calculations and found that he was correct. He concluded that the Moon was pulled round the Earth by a gravitational force between the Earth and the Moon.

UNIVERSAL GRAVITATION

Newton went on to show how gravity pulls the planets around the Sun and developed his law of universal gravitation. This states that there is a force of gravity between every two objects in the universe. However you only feel the pulling force when one is very large, like the Earth, and the other is very small, like all the objects on the Earth, including you.

❙ An engraving of Newton sitting under the famous apple tree.

❙ The planets are pulled around the Sun by the force of gravity.

Glossary

Ancient Greeks – people who lived about two and a half thousand years ago in the area now called Greece. They were probably the first people to ignore superstitions, myths and legends as explanations about the world, and try to explain it from their observations. They did not experiment as they believed this interfered with nature.

air resistance – the force exerted by air as a vehicle or object moves against it.

astronaut – a person who travels and works in space.

axle – the centre-pin around which a wheel spins.

beam – a thick horizontal rod made of wood or metal that can be part of the structure of a building.

bobsleigh – a sledge which can be steered and has a brake. It can be used for racing.

drag – the force of the air as it rushes over a vehicle. Streamlined vehicles create less drag than vehicles with large, flat surfaces.

effort – the force acting on a lever produced by a person or machine which is employed to move the load.

engine – a machine which provides power to move a vehicle such as a car or a spacecraft.

exert – to apply a force.

force meter – a device for measuring the strength of a force in Newtons.

friction – the force which occurs where two objects touch, and where one or more of the objects is moving. If an object is pushed across a surface, and then the pushing force is taken away, the object will continue to move until the force of friction brings it to a stop.

gear wheel – a wheel with teeth around its edge which interlock into the teeth of another gear wheel. It is used to increase the strength of a force or the speed of movement.

gravity – a force exerted by a large body such as the Earth, and which pulls other objects towards its surface.

lever – a simple machine which has a bar and a pivot. The bar turns on the pivot. Levers are used to make lifting and moving objects easier.

load – the force acting on a lever due to the weight of an object.

machine – a device which makes work easier to do.

mass – the amount of matter in something.

matter – the substance which all the things around you, whether they are solid, liquid or gas, are made of.

muscle – a fleshy part of the body which can be contracted (made shorter) to pull on bones in order to move them.

Newton – a unit which is used by scientists when they are measuring forces. It was named after the scientist Isaac Newton.

pivot – the point around which something turns. A lever turns on a pivot, sometimes called a fulcrum.

pulley – a wheel over which a rope is pulled to raise objects. Its use makes lifting objects easier.

sky diver – a person who jumps out of an aircraft and performs acrobatics as he or she falls part of the way through the sky. The sky diver then opens his or her parachute in order to land safely.

sliding friction – the force between two surfaces as they slide over each other.

static friction – the force which keeps an object stationary when a force is pushing on it to try to make it move.

streamlined – being a shape which allows an object to pass easily through air or water.

tread – the pattern on a bike or car tyre. It helps to spray water on the road away from the tyre's surface, so increasing the amount of friction between the tyre and the road.

water resistance – the push of water on an object as the object moves through it.

winch – a simple machine with a handle that is turned to make it rotate and raise or lower a load attached to it.

work – the movement of a force for a distance.

Index

ABOUT THIS BOOK

This aim of this book is to provide information and enrichment for the topic of forces in the Upper Key Stage 2 UK Science Curriculum. There are five lines of scientific enquiry. By reading the book the children are making one of them – research using secondary sources. The text is supported by simple investigations the reader can make to experience what has been described. Many of these investigations are simply illustrative to reinforce what has been read and practise observational skills, but the following investigations are also examples of types of scientific enquiry. Grouping and classifying: page 5; Pattern seeking: pages 7, 11, 21; Comparative test: pages 9, 13, 23, 27; Fair test: 15, 17, 19, 25, 28.